SECRETS OF THE UNEXPLAINED

Paranormal Powers

by Gary L. Blackwood

BENCHMARK BOOKS

MARSHALL CAVENDISH
NEW YORK

Benchmark Books
Marshall Cavendish Corporation
99 White Plains Road
Tarrytown, New York 10591

Library of Congress Cataloging-in-Publication Data
Blackwood, Gary L.
Paranormal powers / Gary L. Blackwood.
p.   cm. — (Secrets of the unexplained)
Includes bibliographical references and index.
Summary: Discusses ESP, enhanced perception, psychokinesis, and other
paranormal phenomena, as well as the work of psychic detectives and water witches.
ISBN 0-7614-0468-6
1. Parapsychology—Juvenile literature. [1. Parapsychology.]
I. Title. II. Series: Blackwood, Gary L. Secrets of the unexplained.
BF1031.B576   1999   133—dc21   97-48478   CIP   AC

Front cover: courtesy of Steven Hunt/The Image Bank; back cover: courtesy of Michel Tcherevkoff/The Image
Bank; pages 6, 36 (top and bottom), 53: Charles Walker Collection/Stock Montage; pages 8-9, 70: Michel
Tcherevkoff/The Image Bank; pages 13 (top and bottom), 63 (top): Dr. Elmar R. Gruber/Fortean Picture
Library; page 16: Duke University Archives; page 21: Russell Targ; page 24, 25, 33: UPI/Corbis-Bettman; page
31: Mark Bourdillon/Rex Features, London; pages 40-41: Archive Photos; page 45: Kevin Braithwaite/Fortean
Picture Library; pages 48, 50, 59: Fortean Picture Library; page 51: Illustrated London News/Archive Photos;
page 57: Guy Lyon Playfair/Fortean Picture Library; page 63 (bottom): Dennis Stacy/Fortean Picture Library;
page 64: Mary Evans Picture Library; page 67: Chris Alan Wilton/The Image Bank

Printed in Hong Kong

3   5   6   4

Contents

Introduction

Let's start with a little experiment.

Put a big glob of Play-Doh over each of your eyes (be sure to close them first) and press it firmly into place. Now stick a six-inch circle of aluminum foil over the Play-Doh. Next wrap a couple of yards of gauze bandage around and around your head to block out all light.

All set? Now read the rest of this page. What do you mean, you can't? Concentrate. Still can't do it? Well, don't feel too bad. Not many people can.

But believe it or not, there are a few who, even with their eyes completely covered this way, can read a book or steer a bicycle through a crowded city street. And that's child's play compared to the powers that some other extraordinary individuals have—powers that science calls paranormal, or beyond the normal.

There are well-documented accounts of people moving or bending solid objects without touching them, projecting their thoughts onto film, stopping their own heartbeat, locating gold mines and

Spoon bending is one paranormal skill that's been mastered by lots of ordinary people. It's hard to imagine a practical use for it, though.

tracking down murderers, describing scenes and events from thousands of miles away, walking barefoot across red-hot lava, even rising from the ground and soaring through the air.

Powers like these fall into two broad categories: 1) mental powers, such as telepathy and remote viewing, and 2) physical powers, such as psychokinesis and levitation. But there's a fine line between the two. Mental powers sometimes produce physical effects, and many physical powers seem to be controlled by the mind.

PART ONE

Mental Powers: The Sixth Sense

Extrasensory Perception

Most of us have little trouble accepting the existence of special mental powers. Look at the classified ads in any popular newspaper or magazine to get a large sampling of the hundreds of thousands of so-called psychics who make a living by using their mental powers. How genuine those powers are depends on the psychic.

Surveys show that a majority of us believe in extrasensory perception (ESP)—the ability to see or feel things without the use of the usual five senses. And, according to one of those surveys, 67 percent of American adults have actually *experienced* ESP.

Certainly we've all heard stories of people who sensed that a friend or family member was in danger. That's called "crisis telepathy." Telepathy is probably the most common form of ESP. It's the transfer of thoughts or mental images from one person to another without speaking.

Clairvoyance, another form of ESP, is the ability to mentally "see" distant objects or events.

In a third kind of ESP, precognition, the psychic person sees events that haven't happened yet. (For more about precognition, see the volume in this series titled *Fateful Forebodings*.)

Parapsychologists, scientists who study the paranormal, have a tough time telling whether a psychic subject is using telepathy or clairvoyance or a combination of the two. So both are usually lumped under a single heading: general ESP, or GESP.

Most parapsychologists think that GESP isn't a rare gift so much as a natural human function—a sixth sense. The theory is that humans once used ESP regularly, to help them survive. But now that life is less challenging, we've lost the ability to use those powers, through lack of practice.

In order for parapsychology to be completely accepted as a "real" science, it has to be able to prove its theories, through testing and experiments. But psychic ability is hard to test accurately. It doesn't obey the traditional rules of science, which say that for an experiment to be valid, it has to be repeatable, with the same results. ESP isn't that reliable. Like inspiration, it comes and goes without warning.

People have been reporting psychic phenomena for thousands of years, but nobody made any effort to study such things systematically until 1882, when a group of English scientists formed the Society for Psychical Research. The SPR's purpose was to investigate such "unscientific" areas as hypnosis, "thought transference" (telepathy), and spiritualism (contacting spirits of the dead).

The SPR's first report was a study of the five Creery sisters, who had a reputation for uncanny telepathic powers. For a year the investigators tested the girls by asking them to identify playing cards or numbers chosen by an investigator in another room.

Monica Tejada, a psychic subject in a 1989 ESP test, demonstrates her ability to "see" words hidden in a sealed box. First she concentrates on the message, then she shows her successful guess—the word truth.

At first the Creerys had an unbelievable success rate. But the longer they were tested, the less accurate they got. Finally investigators caught the sisters giving signals to one another. Though they may have resorted to cheating only because they wanted to repeat their early success, it cast doubt over the whole year's worth of tests.

Another series of tests, done in the United States at Stanford University in the early 1900s, hurt the cause of parapsychology even more. The researchers concluded that none of the subjects they tested showed any evidence of thought transference. That seemed to settle the matter. For the next decade or so, when a person showed unmistakable psychic ability, scientists refused to accept it. One student at Cornell University correctly identified nearly every card in a deck of playing cards, but his professor just scoffed; if the boy were really psychic, he felt, he'd have gotten them all!

But though parapsychology was wounded, it wasn't dead. Individual investigators went on studying and testing ESP. One of the most famous was novelist Upton Sinclair. His 1930 book *Mental Radio* was a nonfiction account of a series of experiments he conducted with his wife, Mary Craig. In these experiments Sinclair concentrated on a simple drawing he'd made, and Mary tried to reproduce it by picking up her husband's mental image. Of the 290 drawings she produced, 65 were totally accurate and another 155 were partially correct.

Scientists dismissed Sinclair's experiments, partly because they weren't carried out in a laboratory, and partly because he hadn't attempted to explain *how* or *why* the process worked.

Hit the Deck

 The same year *Mental Radio* was published, a small group of scientists at Duke University in North Carolina challenged the scientific establishment. The group's leader was J. B. Rhine, now known as the father of modern parapsychology. Like earlier experimenters, he didn't have a theory about what ESP was, but he was determined to find out whether or not it existed.

After searching for some time for a test that was simple and easily controlled, Rhine and his colleagues came up with something called Zener cards, now usually called ESP cards—a deck of twenty-five cards, each with one of five basic symbols: a star, a cross, a circle, a square, or three wavy lines.

Because there are five symbols, if you choose a card at random from an ESP deck, you have one chance in five of guessing what's on it, provided you don't peek—and provided you don't use ESP. Rhine called these one-in-five odds the "mean chance expectation." What his team was looking for was someone who could score well over chance. They found him in a student named Linzmayer, who was really part of a hypnosis experiment. When Rhine idly tested the

J. B. Rhine didn't limit his ESP experiments to humans. In the 1950s he tested a dog named Chris, who was trained to respond to each symbol on Zener cards by pawing a certain number of times. In early experiments, Chris guessed the correct symbol nearly 75 percent of the time.

Zener cards on him, Linzmayer got nine "hits," or correct guesses, in a row. The odds of that happening are about two million to one.

Once Rhine had established Linzmayer's psychic ability, he proceeded to test its limits. He found that when the subject was put under pressure to do well or when he was tired, his scores plummeted. To test the effects of drugs on ESP, Rhine gave Linzmayer a dose of sodium amytal, a mild sedative. Not only did it play havoc with his scores, it put him soundly to sleep.

Concerned about how this might look to a visitor, Rhine shook him more or less awake. With Linzmayer staggering like a drunk, they made their way down to Rhine's car. Rhine drove Linzmayer to the dormitory, half dragged him down the hall while the other students were at supper, and stuck him under a cold shower.

With Linzmayer due to graduate, Rhine's team was forlorn, but they soon found a replacement, a student named Pearce. Pearce scored well consistently, but without the spectacular runs of Linzmayer—until one day Rhine jokingly said, "I'll bet you a hundred dollars you can't get this one."

Pearce got it. Rhine made the same bet on the next card, and the next. Pearce kept winning until the cards ran out—twenty-five hits in a row. Since $2,500 was roughly equal to Rhine's annual salary, Pearce didn't make him pay up. He never again equaled that amazing run. His scores dropped over time, like those of the Creery sisters, until he often scored below average.

In 1934, after three years of research, Rhine published his findings. For the title of his book he used a new term he'd coined: *Extra-Sensory Perception*. The book created a sensation in the scientific world, and brought howls of protest from skeptics. Some suspected Rhine of using sloppy methods, such as shuffling the cards by hand or giving unconscious signals to the subjects. Others accused him of faking the results.

But most scientists saw that Rhine was onto something that deserved further investigation. Rhine continued his experiments,

Are You ESP-Prone?

One of the things Rhine discovered with his experiments is that ESP is really more normal than paranormal; we all have it to some degree. But, as with any other skill, some display more of it than others. In fact there seem to be certain personality types who are ESP-prone, in the way that others are accident-prone. They're likely to score better than average in experiments involving ESP.

How do you know whether or not you're one of them? You can start by taking the following test, based on the findings of Rhine and other parapsychologists. On a sheet of paper, make a column of letters from A to N. Read the questions and write down the number, on a scale of 1 to 5, that best describes your personality. The last four questions have just a yes-or-no answer.

A. Are you more introverted (shy, thoughtful, a loner) or extroverted (outgoing, active, social)?	Introverted				Extroverted
	1	2	3	4	5
B. Are you more practical-minded or imaginative?	Practical				Imaginative
	1	2	3	4	5
C. Are you insensitive or sensitive to the feelings of others?	Insensitive				Sensitive
	1	2	3	4	5
D. Do you place more value on thoughts or feelings?	Thoughts				Feelings
	1	2	3	4	5
E. Do you believe psychic phenomena are common or nonexistent?	Nonexistent				Common
	1	2	3	4	5

but he didn't ignore his critics; he tightened his procedures by putting testers and subjects in separate rooms and using a card-shuffling machine.

In 1957 J. B. Rhine and other parapsychologists formed the Parapsychological Association to promote the study of psychic phe-

F. Do you tend to judge and analyze things and people, or accept them as they are?	Analyze				Accept
	1	2	3	4	5
G. Are you lucky or unlucky?	Unlucky				Lucky
	1	2	3	4	5
H. Do you live in a big city, an isolated area, or somewhere in between?	City				Isolated
	1	2	3	4	5
I. Do you worry a lot, or are you relaxed?	Worry				Relaxed
	1	2	3	4	5
J. When you play cards or board games, do you usually win or lose?	Lose				Win
	1	2	3	4	5
K. Are you left-handed?	Yes				No
L. Are there psychic people in your family?	Yes				No
M. Do you ever have migraine headaches?	Yes				No
N. Are you a girl?	Yes				No

For each *yes*, give yourself a 5. For each *no*, give yourself a 1. Now total all the numbers.

If your total is 57–70, get yourself a crystal ball and go into business.

If you scored 43–56, your sixth sense is strong. Start trusting your hunches.

If you got 29–42, you're no mind reader, but you've got potential.

If your score is 14–28, don't get into any poker games.

nomena. Twelve years later the leading science organization in the United States, the American Association for the Advancement of Science, accepted Rhine's group as a member. That didn't mean that everyone suddenly considered parapsychology a legitimate science, but it did open the way for more researchers.

Remote Chances

 In 1973 Russel Targ and Harold Puthoff, physicists at the Stanford Research Institute in California, began a series of experiments known as Project Scanate. Their purpose was to test a phenomenon they called "remote viewing." Their first subject was a New York artist, Ingo Swann. At first all Swann was asked to do was describe objects hidden inside a wooden box. Swann didn't consider that enough of a challenge. He suggested they give him the coordinates—latitude and longitude—of some distant spot, and he'd try to describe what was there.

Though Puthoff and Targ suspected this was impossible, they went along with the idea and gave Swann the coordinates 49°20' south by 70°14' east. Swann drew a map of an island, complete with geographical and human-built features. Look up those coordinates on a world map or globe; you'll see he was describing the island of Kerguelen.

Theoretically Swann could have had an eidetic, or photographic, memory and memorized a world map. Or he might have gotten the

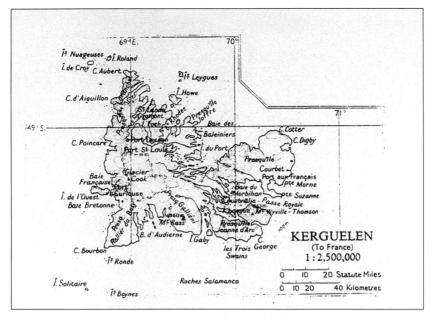

KERGUELEN ISLAND

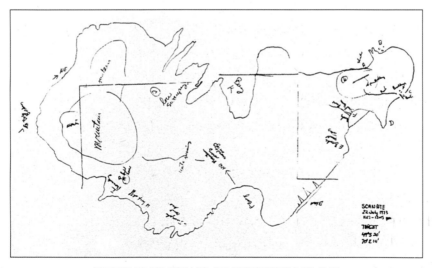

DRAWING BY SWANN OF KERGUELEN ISLAND

The coordinates used to test Ingo Swann's remote-viewing ability lay in the middle of the Indian Ocean, far from any land—except for the tiny island of Kerguelen.

information by ESP from the tester's mind. To rule out these possibilities, Targ and Puthoff set up a double-blind experiment, in which neither Swann nor the tester knew what the target was in advance. The tester drove to a spot at random—a playground, for example, or City Hall—and simply observed it for several minutes. Swann, back in the lab, picked up an image of the target and described it in accurate detail.

The physicists brought in a second subject, a former police commissioner named Pat Price. He proved even more accurate. When he was given a set of coordinates, he wrote a five-page description of what was apparently a small military base, with details as minute as the labels on the file folders.

The Soviet Union was carrying out similar experiments, and this made the United States Central Intelligence Agency nervous. The agency worried that the Soviets would use ESP as a spying tool. The CIA began its own remote-viewing project, called Operation Stargate.

Over the next twenty years the CIA spent $20 million testing sixteen psychics known as the Naturals. At first the results looked promising. One of the Naturals drew diagrams of an experimental Soviet submarine and predicted when it would be in use. Others drew maps of tunnels dug by North Korea near the Demilitarized Zone.

But overall the CIA was disappointed in the experiments. Its study showed that the psychics were right only about 25 percent of the time. In 1995 the CIA shut down the program.

The problem may have been not with the psychics but with the attitude of the testers. Puthoff and Targ felt it was crucial for everyone involved in such experiments to believe that remote viewing really works. And Pat Price was sure that, with the right attitude, anybody could duplicate his success. Targ and Puthoff put his theory to the test, on three subjects with no history of psychic ability. To everyone's surprise, each made several hits. One subject gave five correct descriptions out of nine tries. The scientists concluded that Price was right: Nearly anyone can do remote viewing. What's more, it's a skill that seems to improve with practice.

Another sort of remote viewing, called "eyeless seeing," is much rarer and a lot harder to master. Kuda Bux, the most famous eyeless seer, said it took him eleven years of practice. In the 1930s Bux performed on the stage as the "Man with the X-ray Eyes." With his face covered by layers of flour paste, cotton wads, gauze, and tape, Bux managed to describe objects, copy written messages, read books, ride a bike through Times Square, and walk along a narrow ledge on a high building.

His magician friends wouldn't play cards with him if he was blindfolded, and three female singers refused to take a dressing room next to his. "We would have no privacy," one of them protested. "There is only one brick wall between us and Kuda Bux."

In 1937 *Life* magazine ran a feature on the "*Boy* with the X-ray Eyes," a thirteen-year-old named Pat Marquis. Like Bux, the boy could supposedly read with his eyes bandaged. But when J. B. Rhine and his colleagues tested Marquis, they found he was peeking down

Kuda Bux modestly asserted that anyone could learn to "see with the mind's eye" as he did; it was simply a matter of concentration. Here Bux demonstrates that he can even bat a cricket ball while blindfolded. The gap in the wrapping allowed Bux to breathe, but not to peek. Beneath the bandage, Bux's eyes were covered with coins and tape, or with flour paste.

Teenager Pat Marquis demonstrated some striking powers, such as the ability to see future events and to speak Persian. But, like many psychics, when he was tested he resorted to cheating and damaged his credibility.

alongside his nose, where the bandage didn't fit tightly. Another teenager, Margaret Foos, pulled the same trick on the TV show *People Are Funny* in 1960.

Kuda Bux was tested repeatedly but was never found guilty of such trickery. Bux isn't unique. When Europeans first explored the Samoan Islands in the eighteenth century, they encountered several natives who claimed to be blind but who could describe the visitors in detail.

In the late 1800s Cesare Lombroso, a noted Italian neurologist, tested a fourteen-year-old girl who could read letters and identify colors using not her eyes but, apparently, the tip of her nose and the lobe of one ear.

In the 1920s French doctor Jules Romains tested both blind people and sighted people who were blindfolded, and concluded that microscopic nerve endings in the skin might be able to distinguish between light and dark.

Fifty years later a ten-year-old Polish girl named Bogna Stefanska demonstrated this "skin sight" pretty convincingly; she could sense the color, shape, and size of an object with her fingertips—but without touching the object.

Test Your ESP

 You probably don't care to spend eleven years, as Kuda Bux did, learning to see without eyes. The kind of remote viewing Targ and Puthoff experimented with is much easier. You may want to give it a shot.

First off, you have to be comfortable with the idea. You have to believe it's possible. If you do, here are some tips on successful remote viewing.

- It's best to do the experiment with three people: the viewer, the recorder, and the target. You can do without the recorder if necessary.

- The target chooses a site, without telling the others, and agrees to be there at a specific time and to observe the surroundings for fifteen minutes.

- A few minutes before that time, the viewer sits in a comfortable chair in a quiet room and relaxes, keeping the mind clear. At the chosen time the viewer describes whatever images come to mind. The recorder writes down the descriptions and helps by asking questions about specific features. Don't try to figure out exactly where the target is, just give images and impressions. The viewer can sketch on paper the most important features.

• When the target returns, all three should visit the site and compare the descriptions and sketches with the real thing. The viewer nearly always picks up some "noise"—images that have nothing to do with the target site. But many of the details should match. If not, don't give up. Try again when you're more relaxed, or with friends who are more open to the idea.

If remote viewing just doesn't work for you, you may want to try J. B. Rhine's method of testing ESP with cards. Here's how. Run off five copies of the symbols opposite on a copy machine. Cut out all the symbols and glue them firmly onto the faces of an old deck of playing cards. Shuffle your twenty-five-card deck half a dozen times.

There are several ways to proceed. 1) Guess the order of the cards without touching the deck. 2) Lay the cards out face down, and guess each one in turn. 3) Take the cards off the deck one at a time, and guess each one.

It's best if a friend handles the cards and records your guesses. As with the remote viewing, don't try to figure out what's on each card; just clear your mind and let the images come. The law of "mean chance expectation" says you'll get five hits out of the twenty-five cards. You may score higher or lower on any given run. But if you *consistently* score higher, there's probably ESP at work. If you consistently score below average, you're probably trying too hard; relax. If you're anxious or lack confidence, your ESP may actually be working to avoid getting hits.

Many genuine psychics don't do well with tests like these. They feel it's just a game; there's no real *need* involved. When Rhine and his team tested British psychic Eileen Garrett with ESP cards, she didn't score as high as some of Rhine's students. She was used to working with people, she said, not cards.

Psychic Detectives

 When people with paranormal powers are given something significant and real to do, the results can be astounding. Probably the most controversial and well-publicized role psychics play is in helping to solve crimes. Most major law enforcement agencies have experimented with psychics, and some detectives regularly ask reliable psychics to help put them on the right track in a tough investigation. The FBI has given seminars on "How Psychics Can Be Useful." There are even a couple of organizations—the Psychic Detective Bureau and Professional Psychics United—that specialize in bringing police and psychics together. A Texas detective says that "someday psychics will be part of all larger police departments—it's another tool of the trade, like fingerprinting or photography."

Though "psychic bloodhounds" have just recently started gaining acceptance, they've been around for hundreds of years. In 1692 Jacques Aymar, a dowser (someone with the ability to pinpoint underground deposits of water and minerals), used his dowsing rod to track

Law enforcement agencies often ask psychics to sketch their extrasensory impressions of crime scenes, victims, or suspects.

three men who murdered a French wine merchant. He followed their trail for several days and 150 miles and found one of the culprits in a local jail, where he was being held for some minor crime. The other two escaped over the border into Spain.

In 1928 Maximillian Langsner, a Canadian mind reader, was called in by the Royal Canadian Mounted Police to help solve a murder on a farm in the province of Alberta. The Mounties had a suspect, but no murder weapon. Langsner sat down outside the prisoner's cell and stared at him for five hours, until the psychic got a mental image of where the gun was hidden. The police found the weapon buried in the dirt, right where Langsner said it would be. When they confronted their prisoner with it, he broke down and confessed.

For every case like this, in which using a psychic paid off, there are a dozen total disappointments. Because psychics can report only impressions, not facts, it's often hard for police to sort out the useful information from the useless. And sometimes even useful information is misinterpreted. A Montana sheriff says that "working with a psychic is like doing a crossword puzzle!"

Psychics are the first to admit that they're not always clear or correct. Psychic sleuth John Catchings says, "About twenty percent of the time I'm dead wrong. Another sixty percent I'm only partially right. But on the last twenty percent I'm right on it."

Catchings has been "right on it" often enough to locate the bodies of a dozen or more murder victims and to put the police on the trail of many criminals. He uses a technique called psychometry. When he holds some object—a ring or a piece of clothing, for example—that belonged to the victim, he gets "vibrations" that tell him that person's fate.

New Jersey psychic Dorothy Allison also uses psychometry, but the 1967 case that first made her famous came to her in a dream. Her dream showed the body of a missing five-year-old caught in a drainpipe; a building in the background had the number 8 on it. The boy was dressed in a green snowsuit, and his shoes were on the wrong feet.

She reported her vivid dream to the police. Two months later they found the boy's body in a pond, near Public School No. 8. He wore a green snowsuit, and his sneakers were on the wrong feet.

When Dorothy Allison provides the police with psychic clues, she customarily adds: "I don't know how this will help you—you have to figure it out."

Several large pipes fed water to the pond; police believed the body could have been wedged in one of them before washing into the pond.

Another of Allison's cases had a happier ending. She told the father of a missing eighteen-year-old that his daughter was safe and living in a dirty house with a red door. She saw something about taxis, a street with a president's name, and the numbers 1, 8, and 6. The girl was found in a dirty building that housed a taxi service, just off Monroe Street. The number on the red door was 186.

Allison has a room filled with letters of thanks and honorary police badges. But, like many true psychics, she refuses to accept money for her services. "If I have been blessed with this gift," she says, "it would be wrong to use it for anything but humanitarian purposes."

Sometimes it seems more like a curse than a gift. In 1980, when psychic Etta Smith pinpointed the area in a canyon where the body of a missing nurse could be found, the police charged her with the murder. She was jailed for four days before the real murderer confessed.

Water Witches

 Using psychic powers to find water is a lot less risky than finding murderers. This ability, once called divining or water witching, is now usually referred to as dowsing. And it's used not just to find water, but also to locate minerals and lost objects, to determine the sex of chickens, to hunt deer, to diagnose auto engine problems, even to select vitamins and video rentals.

In fact, dowsing has become something of a fad. The American Society of Dowsers estimates that about two million people in this country use dowsing in various ways.

Dowsing, like psychic crime solving, has a long history. Rock paintings in the Sahara Desert dating from 6000 B.C. show a cattle herder holding a forked stick identical to the traditional dowsing rod. Egyptian sculptures from 2000 B.C. feature a priest using a similar device. In the Middle Ages the church frowned on divining, calling it the work of the devil, so the art more or less disappeared in Europe.

It emerged again in the 1400s, when German miners began using dowsing rods to locate underground minerals. It became an elaborate and fairly respected practice. Dowsers used a different kind

One experienced dowser says that dowsing rods are "like cantankerous children: they won't work unless you ask them to, and certainly won't work if you try and force them to."

Good dowsers consider themselves capable of finding far more than just water. Archaeologists have been known to use dowsing as a way of locating and identifying buried objects, such as this human skull.

of wood for each type of mineral: a rod of hazel wood to find silver, ash wood for copper, pine for lead and tin, and a steel rod for gold. By the eighteenth century German dowsers were being awarded diplomas and were considered more valuable than surveyors.

Then, in the late nineteenth century, people began to look to science to tell them things like where to find minerals and where to drill for water; dowsing fell out of favor again. But when science failed, some people still resorted to the old ways—and not just a few flaky individuals, either. Big corporations and even governments have put dowsers on their payrolls.

Though dowsers traditionally have been men, one of the most famous was a woman, Evelyn Penrose. In the 1930s, as the official dowser of the government of British Columbia, in Canada, she found not only water but copper, silver, lead, gold, and oil. She was accurate more than 90 percent of the time. But, as with ESP, some people weren't impressed with anything less than perfect. If Penrose estimated the depth of a water supply at thirty feet and it came in at twenty-nine, she was called a genius. But if the drillers had to go to thirty-one feet, they wrote letters of complaint to the government.

In 1951 General Motors was building a plant in water-scarce South Africa. When their expert well driller found only saltwater, a GM employee named C. J. Bekker volunteered to dowse a good source of water. He didn't use a dowsing rod; he simply folded his arms across his chest and walked over the property until, in one spot, he began to shake uncontrollably. Though GM officials were skeptical, they took a gamble and drilled in that spot. They struck a supply of water that was more than enough for all their needs.

Occidental Petroleum got its start with ten oil wells that were located by a dowser. Many water and gas companies have taken to locating underground pipes by dowsing with bent welding rods—so many that the American Water Works Association has issued a pamphlet on how to use the technique.

Even the U.S. military has unofficially taken up dowsing. During the Vietnam War Marines found that, using bent coat hangers, they could locate Vietcong tunnels, booby traps, and even minefields.

There have been countless attempts to explain how dowsing works. Eighteenth-century English surgeon William Pryce suggested that tiny particles rise up from underground deposits of water or minerals and enter the tip of the dowsing rod, weighing it down so that it dips earthward. A century later Irish scientist William Barrett stated that dowsing must use some form of mental powers.

Skeptics have always claimed that the dowser is unconsciously reading the lay of the land and just guessing at spots where water is most likely to be found.

The most popular theory among scientists is that large deposits of water or minerals cause a change in the earth's magnetic field and that this affects the electrical impulses in our brains; as a result our muscles twitch involuntarily, and the movement is amplified by the dowsing instrument.

A good theory—if the only things dowsing could locate were water and minerals. But some dowsers regularly use their skills to find missing people or lost objects by holding a pendulum over a map. Sometimes they ask the pendulum questions and watch how it responds. (See *Fateful Forebodings* in this series for more on this technique.) It's hard to imagine how magnetic forces could account for that.

Probably only 5 to 10 percent of us have a strong natural talent for dowsing. But most studies show that with practice nearly anyone can learn to dowse accurately. Experienced dowsers use all sorts of devices—plastic tubing, pennies, pendulums, even a Polish sausage bent in a semicircle. The best bet for a beginner is a pair of wire rods cut from coat hangers.

Bend each rod into an L shape; the long side of the L should be about fourteen inches, the short side about five inches. When you're ready to use your homemade rods, find an area of open ground. Hold the short sides of the rods like two six-guns; grasp them firmly but not tightly. Keeping the long sides parallel to the ground, walk around. When you pass over a buried electrical cable or a water pipe or a drain, the rods should react, either by crossing or by swinging apart. You can make the rods do this by tilting your hands, but you'll know the real thing when it happens because you'll have a hard time making the rods point straight ahead.

If you want to locate something specific, the trick is to focus on that particular thing so the rods don't react to everything you pass over. As with remote viewing and ESP, it's important to believe dowsing will work, and to stay relaxed. Don't try to control the rods. As British dowser Tom Graves says, "Treat the instrument as if it has a life and mind of its own."

PART TWO

Physical Powers: Mind

Over

Matter

A Potpourri of Powers

Though most of us can learn to dowse or to do remote viewing, there are other paranormal powers that are beyond our reach. Some of them you probably wouldn't really care to have anyway.

It might be useful to be a "human cork" like Angelo Faticoni, who could float in the water even with a twenty-pound cannonball lashed to his legs; of course, it would be unhandy if you wanted to go scuba diving.

And if you could make your chickens lay eggs with pictures on them, as Gertrude Smith did, it might turn into a moneymaking business.

If you had Tom Wiggins's ability, you'd never have to take piano lessons. The blind black man, who lived in the late 1800s, could flawlessly play any piano piece, no matter how complex, after hearing it performed once or twice. He even copied exactly the style of the performer.

And if you were like Lulu Hurst, you wouldn't need karate

lessons. Late in the nineteenth century Hurst had a brief performing career as "the Georgia Wonder." The frail fourteen-year-old could fling three grown men around the stage with no effort, using what she called simply the Power.

But chances are you wouldn't be so happy to have some of the other strange powers that people have been blessed—or plagued—with. It would be inconvenient, to say the least, to be Jacqueline Priestman; she has so much static electricity in her body that she burns out electrical appliances, and her TV set changes channels whenever she gets near it.

Or imagine being Jennie Morgan, whose handshake delivered an electric shock that knocked people unconscious. Or Peter Strickland, whose presence makes computers and calculators go haywire. Or physicist Wolfgang Pauli who, when he walked into a laboratory, caused pieces of lab equipment to tumble off shelves and shatter.

Even worse, you could be like Bendetto Supino, the nine-year-old Italian boy whose bedclothes and furniture and comic books burst into flame when he stared at them.

And then there are the folks with "magnetic personalities." In the wake of the accident at the Soviet nuclear power plant at Chernobyl, a disturbing number of Russians have reported a newfound ability to make frying pans and irons and silverware stick to their bodies. Some even attract glass and plastic as well as metal. American Frank McKinstry was reportedly so magnetic that if he stood still, his feet stuck to the earth and had to be pried loose.

It's hard to imagine anyone wanting to duplicate the feats of

Russian parapsychologist Edward Naumov got silverware to stick to this subject. But when the subject tried to attract metal later, on his own, it just wouldn't stick to him.

Mirin Dajo. The Dutch mystic regularly allowed a sword to be driven through his body, with no lasting injury. When skeptics said it must be an illusion, Dajo used an open-ended hollow sword and pumped water through it to show that the entire blade passed through his body. He repeated his daring demonstration some five hundred times before he died—as a result of one of the sword wounds.

Defying Gravity

 The ability to fly seems much more appealing. But for those who have actually had that power, it often proved a source of embarrassment rather than delight.

Levitating, or floating in the air, isn't as rare a feat as you might expect. In fact there are hundreds of reports of levitations. Many are just legends, but some are well documented, by very reliable witnesses. The majority of cases involve priests, monks, and nuns, some of whom were later declared saints by the church.

The most spectacular example by far was Joseph of Copertino, a seventeenth-century Italian monk known as the Flying Friar. At the age of seventeen Joseph became a novice monk, but he was so clumsy and absentminded that the monastery threw him out. In 1625 he was accepted by the Franciscans. He was so determined to give up worldly pleasures that he wore a scratchy hair shirt and sprinkled his food with bitter powder so he wouldn't enjoy eating it.

One worldly thing he did enjoy was music. At a Christmas Eve service, while listening to shepherds playing their pipes, Joseph was

Witnesses who saw the Flying Friar levitate claimed that during his flights his robe stayed perfectly in place. Once, the friar landed amid burning candles on the altar of a church, but the flames failed to scorch him or his clothing.

carried away—literally. With a sharp cry, he rose into the air and flew twenty yards across the church to the altar.

Nature also made him flighty. One day as he was admiring the monastery garden, he gave that same high-pitched cry and flew to the top of an olive tree. Unfortunately the power then deserted him; his companion had to fetch a ladder and help him down.

On other occasions Joseph grabbed a fellow monk and lifted him aloft, too. His superiors were not amused by his aerial antics, which often interrupted Mass. After he rose in the air at a meal, waving a piece of fish, he was forced to eat alone.

When people began turning up hoping to see him fly, Joseph was sent away to another monastery. There, too, the public heard of his powers and came to gawk. The wife of the Spanish ambassador was so astounded that she fainted. The duke of Brunswick was so impressed that he converted to Catholicism.

Joseph was transferred again and again, always with the same results. Over a period of thirty years he levitated at least a hundred times before thousands of witnesses. Eventually he was brought before Pope Urban VIII. Joseph was so overcome by the honor that he rose in the air and hung there until he was ordered to come down.

In 1663 Joseph performed one last levitation. As he lay dying, his body rose "about a palm's width" and hovered before his startled doctors.

Teresa of Avila, a nun who lived about a hundred years before Joseph, was more disturbed by her unusual power. "I confess that it threw me into a great fear . . . ," she wrote, "for when I saw my body thus lifted up from the earth, how could I help it?"

Not everyone who can levitate is so reluctant, or so religious. The Scottish-American psychic D. D. Home showed off his ability many times, before the likes of Napoleon III and Mark Twain. In 1868 Lord Adare and friends watched openmouthed as Home sailed out one window of Adare's apartment—seventy feet above the ground—and in again through another window.

In this photo Amedee Zuccarini looks as if he merely could be leaping off the table. But witnesses said he stayed aloft for twelve to fourteen seconds.

The friends of Italian psychic Amedee Zuccarini took flash photographs of him as he floated off the floor; the pictures were published in a scientific journal in 1908. In the 1970s followers of Maharishi Mahesh Yogi, founder of Transcendental Meditation, claimed the yogi had taught them to levitate. They, too, produced photos, but never gave a public demonstration of their powers.

Though Indian yogic teachings include instructions on how to levitate, many so-called levitations are probably just illusions. Note the upright staff relied on by this yogi.

Burning Questions

Remember Kuda Bux, the "Man with the X-ray Eyes"? In 1935 he tried to prove that his powers went beyond just eyeless seeing. He had a twenty-foot trench dug at Rockefeller Center in New York City and filled with red-hot coals. Then he proceeded to walk barefoot over them. After hotfooting it for only ten feet, he had to leap out of the pit. Though the soles of Bux's feet came through without a blister or burn, his short stroll wasn't very impressive compared with the feats of other fire-walkers.

Fire-walking has been a hot item since at least the time of ancient Rome. It's an art that's practiced all over the world, too, from India to Africa to Eastern Europe. Some cultures use burning coals, some use white-hot stones. In Hawaii priests saunter barefoot along rivers of fresh volcanic lava.

During an annual celebration in Lankadas, Greece, a group of dancers, after several hours of meditation, jump into a pit filled with coals as hot as 850 degrees Fahrenheit. For half an hour or so they

Fire-walking seems contrary to the laws of physics. But one writer on the paranormal points out that "there are other, equally valid definitions of reality, and in one of these this procedure of 'fire-walking' is possible."

cavort on the coals, until they're reduced to ashes—the coals, that is.

According to the chief fire-walker, the trick lies in believing that it's possible. "Once guided by faith and concentration, the actual dancing on the burning coals is painless. You feel something but it is no more than like walking in a prickly field."

Fiji Islanders who do a similar dance on hot stones believe that their water god spreads "water babies" over the stones for the dancers to walk on. Here, too, the right attitude is crucial. A dancer who failed to prepare himself mentally for the ordeal burned his legs so badly that they had to be amputated.

Though the fire-walkers themselves say it's a matter of mental attitude, scientists offer other explanations. One theory is that the feet of the fire-walkers sweat, and the sweat vaporizes, forming a thin cushion of air between foot and fire. Does this mean that anyone with sweaty feet can fire-walk? Not likely.

One physicist claims that if the walker steps quickly enough, the foot doesn't get hot enough to burn. In fact, his theory says, the feet may actually cool down the burning coals. Obviously he's never gone barefoot on the beach on a scorching summer day.

In any case, neither of these explanations accounts for such "fire kings" as Julian Chabert and Nathan Coker. Chabert, a nineteenth-century Frenchman, could sit in a heated oven holding a leg of lamb until the meat was fully cooked.

Coker, a Maryland slave, found that being fireproof had its advantages. As a child he'd sneak into the kitchen and grab dumplings out of the boiling dinner pot. Later, when he became a blacksmith, he found he didn't need tongs to handle red-hot metal.

"I often take my iron out of the forge with my hand . . . ," he said, "but it don't burn."

If he felt like showing off, Coker would touch his tongue to a heated shovel or scoop up molten lead in his hands and hold it in his mouth until it solidified. He didn't have to wait for his coffee to cool down, either. "I drink my coffee when it is boiling . . . I always likes it just as hot as I can get it."

D. D. Home, the psychic you met earlier, could do more than fly in and out of windows. He could plunge his face into a bed of burning coals, "as though bathing it in water," and carry the glowing embers around in his hands or his shirt pocket.

It's easy to scoff at examples that took place a hundred years ago or more. But there are more recent cases of "fire immunity" that are harder to dismiss. In 1959 a psychiatrist observed members of the Free Pentecostal Holiness Church in Tennessee playing with fire. While in a kind of trance, they held the flame from a homemade kerosene lamp against their hands or feet, even their faces, hair, and clothing, without suffering any burns. One especially daring man cupped a flaming chunk of coal in his hands for over a minute.

Don't even think of trying such a stunt. No matter how sweaty your palms are, a hot coal is guaranteed to roast them like Chabert's leg of lamb. The same goes for any of those other feats involving fire, swords, or cannonballs. They're just too dangerous.

Mind-Bending

Aside from eyeless seeing, the paranormal power that seems to require the most practice and the most concentration is psychokinesis, or PK—the ability to mentally alter physical objects. PK is a much rarer talent than ESP and, while ESP works best if you don't try to force it, PK takes some serious effort.

PK falls into two categories. The type that scientists study most is called micro-PK; it involves using the mind to affect sensitive electronic devices. You can't see micro-PK at work; you can only measure it statistically. Macro-PK is more dramatic. It actually moves objects around or bends them out of shape.

PK has drawn more fire from skeptics than any other brand of psychic power. And the target of much of that skepticism has been a flamboyant Israeli psychic named Uri Geller.

Geller has, or claims to have, a wide array of psychic talents, including telepathy, thought projection (onto film), locating coal and oil, remote viewing, clairvoyance, and teleportation (mentally moving objects over long distances). But he's best known for the rather impractical ability to bend spoons just by holding them, or by rubbing them gently with one finger.

Scientists who tested famed spoon bender Uri Geller admitted that he demon-strated strong ESP. But Geller wasn't satisfied. Anyone could do ESP, he said. He wanted science to confirm his psychokinetic powers.

He displayed this curious ability from the age of five; for years he had trouble eating because the handles of his silverware kept warping. He could also make the hands of his watch move around in either direction and could toss a basketball through a hoop without looking.

In the late 1960s Geller started performing for nightclub audiences in Israel. His act included bending keys and spoons and copying concealed drawings. He became such a sensation that Prime Minister Golda Meir, when asked about Israel's future, replied sarcastically, "I don't know, ask Uri Geller."

In the early seventies Geller took his act on the road and became even more famous in Europe, America, and Japan. His appearances on TV triggered an epidemic of "Geller mania." Floods of calls came in from viewers whose kitchen utensils, rings, and knitting needles had twisted out of shape and whose stopped watches had suddenly started running while they were watching Geller perform.

Even more surprising, hundreds of viewers discovered spoon-bending powers of their own. Some could do it only during Geller's show. Others, mostly children, kept the ability for a long time afterward.

To these "mini-Gellers," the skill seemed simple enough. "I tell it to bend and I think bend," said an eleven-year-old spoon bender. "I say it over and over again to myself while I'm rubbing with my fingers." But it did take a lot of concentration. Most felt exhausted afterward. And the power didn't always work. One thirteen-year-old girl couldn't concentrate with her little brother in the room.

A twelve-year-old Scottish lass named Fiona tried hard to demonstrate her newfound ability before a team of scientists at Edinburgh University but failed miserably. After the session, as she sat glumly next to her scolding mother, staring at the spoons that had betrayed her, one of them suddenly went limp and bent over like a dead flower.

Geller's showy performances brought a barrage of accusations from scientists. Geller himself added to the controversy by making outrageous claims; at one point he revealed that his powers were given to him by an extraterrestrial intelligence called Spectra.

Geller agreed to be tested by a dozen or so laboratories, but he was obviously more interested in amazing others with his powers than in being a scientific guinea pig. When Puthoff and Targ, the physicists who were testing remote viewing, brought Geller to their California lab, he insisted on proving himself by driving blindfolded at high speeds through the streets of Palo Alto.

In keeping with his flair for the dramatic, Geller decorated his Cadillac with five thousand pieces of bent cutlery, including a seven-hundred-year-old Tibetan spoon.

During the six weeks Puthoff and Targ tested Geller, he did some pretty impressive stuff. But most of it wasn't under controlled conditions. When he was asked to mentally move the needle of a magnetometer, a device that measures magnetic fields, he bent the ink pens in the instrument so badly that they leaked red ink all across the graph paper. He moved the picture on a TV monitor right off the screen by shouting, "Up! Down!" He also demonstrated his specialty, bending metal objects, but he could do it only if he touched the objects, which led to suspicion that he was using physical force or perhaps some chemical substance that weakened the metal. The physicists concluded that Geller "possibly" had psychokinetic powers. But "possibly" isn't good enough for science.

In 1973 magician James Randi accused Geller of being a fraud and proceeded to show that he could do most of the things Geller did by using stage tricks. Geller's reputation rapidly went downhill.

But of course the fact that some of Geller's feats could be duplicated by trickery doesn't necessarily prove that Geller used those methods. Many psychics, with pressure on them to perform, have resorted to tricks when their real powers failed. Geller may have done so, too.

It seems clear, though, that spoon bending, at least, is no trick but a genuine phenomenon that's been experienced by hundreds of people. In some areas of the country spoon-bending parties have become a popular pastime. Television executive Diana Gazes found that in her weekly PK workshops about 80 percent of her would-be spoon benders could accomplish it on the first try. Kids are especially successful, probably because, as one young girl put it, "nobody's told us we can't do it."

If you have some old spoons you don't mind messing up, you can have your own PK party. Sit in a circle with several friends, each holding a spoon. Focus on a point inside your head; move the point of concentration down your neck, through your arm, and into the handle of the spoon. Order the spoon to bend. You'll probably feel a little silly; that's normal. Just tell yourself it can be done. You may feel the handle becoming so soft and warm that you can twist or bend it easily. If you really concentrate, and rub the handle with your other hand, the spoon may bend on its own.

Moving Experiences

Though spoon bending is a "hands-on" sort of skill, it may be possible—for a few people, anyway—to perform PK without touching anything. The feat has even been captured on film. Zhang Baosheng, called China's Uri Geller, has been filmed by a high-speed motion picture camera as he moved objects—including live insects—into and out of sealed containers. The process was so quick that observers couldn't see exactly how it happened. But according to a Chinese science magazine, one bit of film footage, when examined frame by frame, shows an object—a pill—actually moving *through* the glass of the container.

In 1967 a Russian woman, Nina Kulagina, was filmed by noted parapsychologist Gaither Pratt as she moved a small cylinder about inside a glass container. On another occasion, when she was asked to move the needle of a compass, she made the whole compass dance around.

Scientists not only tested Kulagina's PK powers, they monitored her body functions as she performed. Her heartbeat sometimes soared

Psychics have been known to bend forks, too.

Kids seem to get the hang of bending metal more easily than adults. This paperweight in a laboratory at the University of London contains a tangle of paper clips mentally mangled by children.

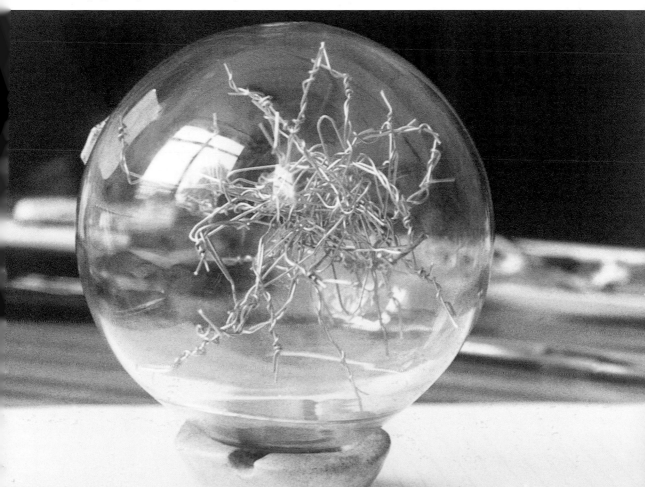

PK requires an extraordinary amount of concentration. Polish medium Stanislawa Tomczyk performed PK best while under hypnosis.

to 240 beats per minute—over three times the normal rate. Her blood sugar and blood pressure rose. During one half-hour PK session she lost two pounds of body weight. Obviously Kulagina had to work hard to produce PK.

Does this mean that there's some sort of physical force involved? Possibly. The scientists found that when Kulagina was moving objects, a magnetic field surrounded her that was ten times normal. The film on some of the cameras in the room fogged up, as if it had been exposed to light. When another Russian psychic, Alla Vinogradova, was performing PK, electrical sparks reportedly shot from her fingers toward the object she was moving.

This seems to indicate that there's some form of electricity at work. You can demonstrate a similar phenomenon yourself by running a comb through your hair on a dry day and picking up tiny scraps of paper with the static-charged comb.

You'd need an awful lot of static electricity, though, to move around a block of wood, a salt shaker, or a compass, as Kulagina and others have done. Where do they get that kind of power?

Some experiments show that when PK is being performed, the temperature of the laboratory can drop as much as ten degrees Fahrenheit. When heat is lost, it means a loss of energy. This suggests that psychics could somehow be absorbing that energy and directing it to move objects.

Altering Atoms

 Scientists have traditionally recognized four basic forces in the world: nuclear, gravitational, radioactive, and electromagnetic. A lot of scientists think that paranormal phenomena, including ESP, must be produced by electromagnetic energy. But it's been demonstrated many times that psychic powers continue to work even when the subject is inside a metal grid called a Faraday cage that blocks out most of the electromagnetic spectrum. That leads parapsychologists to speculate that there's a fifth force in the world, one they call psi, after the letter of the Greek alphabet that begins the word *psyche*, meaning soul or mind.

Quantum physics, which studies the behavior of subatomic particles, offers yet another possibility. Quantum physicists have found that subatomic particles, like psychic powers, don't always follow the same rules as the larger world that we can see and touch. Two odd facts about subatomic behavior may shed some light on how ESP and PK work:

1. Quantum physicists have noted that the very act of observing a

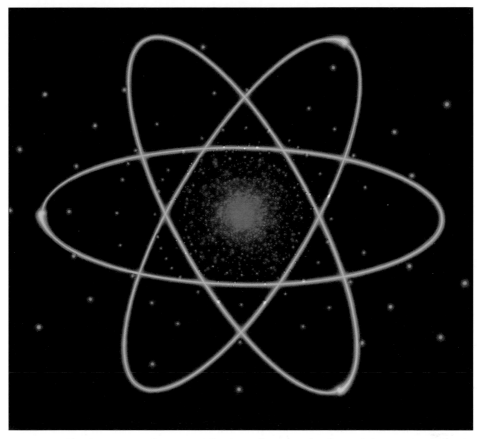

Is it possible that PK and ESP work at a subatomic level? In laboratory tests some subjects have been able to mentally influence the behavior of electrons.

subatomic particle can have an effect on how it behaves. This suggests that if the human mind could influence those subatomic particles enough—get them all moving in the same direction, for instance—it could affect the atoms themselves, and the objects that the atoms are part of.

2. When two subatomic particles split off from an atom, changing the behavior of one particle can affect the behavior of the other one

some distance away. Or, as Puthoff and Targ put it, "parts of the universe apparently separated from each other can nonetheless act together as parts of a larger whole." This could explain how an event is able to impress itself upon the mind of a person who's too far away to see or hear it.

If subatomic particles are dependent upon one another this way, then it's not a big leap to imagine that maybe everything in the universe is somehow connected. It's entirely possible, then, that we humans, rather than being a bunch of separate, unconnected individuals, may be more like cells of one huge organism, or fingers on a cosmic hand: Wiggle one finger, and its neighbor moves, too.

That still doesn't explain exactly how the mental and physical powers you've read about actually work. But the fact that we don't completely understand something certainly isn't reason enough to conclude that it doesn't exist or that it's just a lot of trickery. There was a time, after all, when hypnotism was considered just a magician's trick; now it's a legitimate scientific tool.

If we all really do have some measure of paranormal power, as parapsychologists indicate, it seems a shame not to use it. The fact is, most of us do try to use it sometimes, without quite realizing it. Have you ever tried to guide a bowling ball into hitting that last bowling pin or a pool ball into a pocket by using "body English" or by talking to it? Have you ever whacked or yelled at a vending machine or a lawn mower that refused to work? Have you ever tried to coax a pair of dice to turn up a certain number? Or tried to court good luck and ward off bad luck by carrying around a good luck charm?

When you do such things, you're making a completely illogical attempt to influence the world around you. ESP and PK are completely illogical, too. But for some people, at least, they do seem to work. And who knows—maybe with a little practice you could learn to make them work for you.

The first step, as all those parapsychologists and psychics keep reminding us, is to have an open mind. Or as author Richard Bach says, "Let's pretend it is possible, and see what happens."

Glossary

booby trap: A concealed device designed to injure or kill an enemy; for example, an explosive triggered by a trip wire.

Central Intelligence Agency (CIA): A government agency that collects information about the activities of foreign governments that might threaten the security of the United States.

Chernobyl: Nuclear power plant located eighty miles north of the Ukrainian city of Kiev. It was the site of the worst nuclear reactor accident in history on April 26, 1986.

Demilitarized Zone (DMZ): A 2 1/2-mile-wide strip of land that, since the Korean War (1950–1953), has separated the communist state of North Korea from the democratic Republic of South Korea.

eidetic memory: The ability to call to mind a remembered image with photographic clarity and accuracy.

electromagnetic energy: Energy made up of waves that are both electric and magnetic. Depending on the length and frequency of the waves, the energy can take the form of infrared radiation, visible light, ultraviolet light, X rays, or gamma rays.

Fiji Islands: A group of more than eight hundred islands in the Pacific Ocean, thirteen hundred miles northeast of New Zealand.

latitude and longitude: Measurements used to locate a particular spot on the earth's surface. Latitude tells how far north or south of the equator the spot is; longitude tells how far east or west it is of the prime meridian, an imaginary line that runs through Greenwich, England. Both are measured in degrees (°) and minutes (').

mean chance expectation: On an ESP test, the number of correct guesses a subject can be expected to score purely by chance.

mystic: A person who claims to understand things that are mysteries to ordinary humans.

Napoleon III: Emperor of France 1852–1870.

neurologist: A doctor who specializes in diseases of the nervous system.

parapsychology: The branch of science that studies psychic phenomena such as extrasensory perception and psychokinesis.

pendulum: A heavy object suspended from a string so that it swings freely in response to a movement or force.

Pope Urban VIII: Head of the Roman Catholic Church 1623–1644.

psychometry: Determining facts about an object or its owner just by touching the object.

quantum physics: The branch of science that studies the behavior of sub-atomic particles (see *subatomic particles*).

remote viewing: Receiving mental images of a distant place or object.

Samoan Islands: A group of fifteen volcanic islands in the Pacific Ocean, 2,700 miles east of Australia.

Sinclair, Upton: American writer best known for his novel *The Jungle* (1906), which exposed conditions in the meatpacking industry.

sodium amytal: A mild narcotic drug used to relieve pain or induce sleep.

static electricity: An electric charge that builds up in certain materials or in the air. It "zaps" you when you touch metal after sliding across a fabric car seat, for example. Lightning is a more violent form.

subatomic particles: The smallest known elements of matter, also called fundamental particles. Some familiar examples are photons, electrons, protons, and neutrons.

Transcendental Meditation: A nonreligious method of finding peace and relaxation by disciplining the mind and the body.

To Learn More about Paranormal Powers

BOOKS – NONFICTION

Aylesworth, Thomas G. *ESP.* New York: Franklin Watts, 1975. Discusses the three forms of extrasensory perception, plus psychokinesis. Imaginative illustrations.

Landau, Elaine. *ESP.* Brookfield, Connecticut: Millbrook Press, 1996. A short introduction to the various kinds of extrasensory perception, plus an ESP test.

BOOKS – FICTION

Dahl, Roald. *Matilda.* New York: Puffin, 1990. A young genius discovers psychokinetic powers and uses them to battle the horrid Miss Trunchbull. A 1996 movie version is available on video.

Roberts, Willo Davis. *The Girl with the Silver Eyes.* New York: Scholastic, 1980. Ten-year-old Katie's psychic abilities make her feel "different," and she searches for others who are like her.

Sleator, William. *Into the Dream.* New York: Dutton, 1979. Suspenseful story of a boy and girl who share the same vivid dream.

ORGANIZATIONS

American Society for Psychical Research, 5 West 73rd Street, New York, NY 10023. Investigates and provides information and speakers on all types of psychic phenomena.

American Society of Dowsers, P.O. Box 24, Brainerd Street, Danville, VT 05828. Promotes teaching of dowsing methods. Seventy-five regional groups; annual convention and workshop in August/September.

Professional Psychics United, 7115 West North Avenue, Oak Park, IL 60302. Offers educational programs on ESP.

Index

Page numbers for illustrations are in bold face

Notes

Quotes used in this book are from the following sources:

Page 17 "I'll bet you a hundred dollars": *New Frontiers of the Mind: The Story of the Duke Experiments*, by J. B. Rhine (New York: Farrar, 1937), p. 94.

Page 23 "We would have no privacy": *Psychic Powers*, by the Editors of Time-Life Books (Alexandria, Virginia: Time-Life, 1987), p. 109.

Page 30 "someday psychics will be": "Clairvoyant Crime Busters," by Richard and Joyce Wolkomir, *McCall's*, October 1987, p. 164.

Page 32 "working with a psychic": "Clairvoyant Crime Busters," p. 164.

"About twenty percent": "Clairvoyant Crime Busters," p. 164.

Page 33 "I don't know": "Clairvoyant Crime Busters," p. 164.

Page 34 "If I have been blessed": *Mysteries of the Unexplained*, by the Editors of Reader's Digest (Pleasantville, New York: Reader's Digest, 1982), p. 97.

Page 36 "like cantankerous children": *Dowsing: The Psi Connection*, p. 80.

Page 39 "Treat the instrument": *Dowsing: The Psi Connection*, by Francis Hitching (Garden City, New York: Anchor, 1978), p. 80.

Page 49 "about a palm's width": *The Psychic Reader*, by Martin Ebon (New York: World, 1969), p. 73.

"I confess that it threw": *Mysteries of the Unexplained*, p. 285.

Page 53 "there are other": *Alternate Realities: The Search for the Full Human Being*, by Lawrence LeShan (New York: M. Evans, 1976), p. 24.

Page 54 "Once guided by faith": *Mysteries of the Unexplained*, p. 262.

Page 55 "I often take": *Mysteries of the Unexplained*, p. 266.

"I drink my coffee": *Mysteries of the Unexplained*, p. 266.

"as though bathing": *Mysteries of the Unexplained*, p. 265.

Page 58 "I don't know": *The Geller Effect*, by Uri Geller and Guy Lyon Playfair (New York: Holt, 1986), p. 193.

"I tell it to bend": *Superminds*, by John Taylor (New York: Viking, 1975), p. 63.

Page 60 "nobody's told us": *The Geller Effect*, p. 239.

Page 68 "parts of the universe": *Mind-Reach: Scientists Look at Psychic Ability*, by Russel Targ and Harold E. Puthoff (New York: Delacorte, 1977), p. 170.

Page 69 "Let's pretend it is": *Mind-Reach*, p. xxv.

About the Author

Gary L. Blackwood is a novelist and playwright who specializes in historical topics. His interest in the Unexplained goes back to his childhood, when he heard his father tell a story about meeting a ghost on a lonely country road.

Though he has yet to see a single UFO or ghost, a glimpse of the future or a past life, the author is keeping his eyes and his mind open. Gary lives in Missouri with his wife and two children.